VIA FOLIOS 60

SICILIANA

SICILIANA
BILINGUAL POEMS BY
EMANUEL DI PASQUALE

ILLUSTRATIONS BY
ROCCO CAFISO

EDITED BY
SALVATORE LICITRA

BORDIGHERA PRESS

Library of Congress Control Number: 2009908470

©2009 by Emanuel di Pasquale.

All rights reserved. Parts of this book may be reprinted only by written permission from the author, and may not be reproduced for publication in book, magazine, or electronic media of any kind, except in quotations for purposes of literary reviews by critics.

Printed in the United States.

Published by
Bordighera, Inc.
John D. Calandra Italian American Institute
25 West 43rd Street, 17th Floor
New York, NY 10036

VIA Folios 60
ISBN 1-59954-010-X
ISBN 978-1-59954-010-8

To Anthony Julian Tamburri

CONTENTS

Siciliana 11
Siciliana 13

Elegy 15
Elegia 17

Letter from Sicily 21
Lettera dalla Siciliana 23

Transmutations 25
Trasformazioni 25

The Nature of Pain 27
La natura del dolore 27

It was no dream 29
Non fu sogno 31

Take the song 33
La canzone 35

The Poet Dreams of Being Water 37
Il poeta sogna d'esser acqua 37

Why Complain 39
Perchè lamentarmi 41

Sunset 43
Tramonto 43

SICILIANA

Siciliana

From any point on the hill,
you will smile at the cemetery,
knowing you, too,
will be buried where your father
and your mother are buried.
The black iron gates
and the swirling cypresses
won't frighten you a bit.
The large stars will slowly
roll over your head.
You will suddenly remember the river,
miles from the village,
and stopping to drink at a horse trough,
you will walk for miles into the valley,
and once again you will find the white stones,
the pools of water,
the water bugs swimming their staccato strokes,
the crickets scraping their manic symphonies,
the hermit hauling his bamboo sticks,
and you will follow him
and be his brother.

Siciliana

Da ogni punto della collina,
sorriderai al cimitero,
conoscendoti, inoltre,
sarai sepolto dove tuo padre
e tua madre sono sepolti.
Il nero cancello di ferro
e i turbinanti cipressi
non ti spaventeranno per niente.
Le grande stelle rolleranno lentamente
sopra la tua testa.
All'improvviso ricorderai il fiume,
a mille miglia dal paese,
sostando per bere a un trogolo di cavalli,
camminerai per mille miglia nella valle,
e ancora una volta troverai la bianca pietra,
gli stagni,
gli insetti d'acqua che nuotano con bracciate lente,
i grilli stridenti le loro pazze sinfonie,
l'eremita che trascina i suoi bastoni di bambù
e lo seguirai
e sarai suo fratello.

Elegy

My father walked
through fields of wheat
and roads of stone.
He waded through rivers
and caught eels and small
crabs for our supper.
In the gleaning season,
he filled burlap bags
with almonds and chestnuts;
with cupped hands,
he drank
from mountain springs,
and he rested under
the carob and olive tree,
his pillow the memory
of his wife and children.
And as he rolled
into silent sleep,
my father
put a bird's tongue in my mouth
and gave me song.

Elegia

Mio padre camminava
per i campi di grano
e le strade di pietra.
Egli guadava i fiumi
e prendeva le anguille e i piccoli
granchi per la nostra cena.
Nella stagione della spigolatura,
riempiva i sacchi di tela
di mandorle e castagne;
con le mani a conca
egli beveva
dalle sorgenti di montagna,
e si fermava sotto
il carrubo e l'olivo,
suo cuscino il ricordo
della moglie e dei figli.
E come si rotolò
muto nel sonno,
mio padre
mise una lingua d'uccello
nella mia bocca
e mi diede un canto.

SICILIANA

Letter from Sicily

We haven't stolen the grape from
the vineyard by the sea.
That creek where we used to wash
the stolen grape is now dry;
the water loses itself
in the fields.
This summer even the hunt has grown stale.
Perhaps the rabbits have all hopped
to America to taunt hunters
braver than our hunters.
Return, dear friend,
for one more feast
on a hill,
under the stars,
where we may watch our children dance.

SICILIANA

Lettera dalla Sicilia

Non abbiamo rubato l'acino
dal vigneto sul mare.
L'insenatura dove solevamo lavare
l'acino rubato ora è secca,
l'acqua si perde
nei campi.
Questa estate anche la caccia è sospesa.
Forse i conigli sono saltati
in America per schernire cacciatori
più bravi dei nostri.
Ritorna, caro amico,
per una festa ancora
su un colle,
sotto le stelle,
dove possiamo guardare le nostre danze familiari.

Transmutations

1.

Scarf after scarf,
the ocean unfolds —
what silver cloth.
What white fringes.

2.

All fires take flight into butterflies.

Trasformazioni

1.

Solco dopo solco
l'oceano si apre —
che tessuto d'argento.
Che bianchi ornamenti.

2.

Tutti fuochi trasformati in farfalle.

The Nature of Pain

God, was it you I saw
hunched on a branch,
a snow-clawed thing,
piping low
from under a broken wing?

La Natura del Dolore

Dio, eri tu che io vidi
curvato su di un ramo,
creatura graffiata dalla neve,
che cantavi piano
da sotto un'ala spezzata?

It Was No Dream

It was no dream.
We would embrace.
You nestled your body
against mine,
arms over arms,
your head over my heart,
your sweet scent.
What has happened?
Where are you?

Non fu sogno

Non fu sogno.
Ci abbracciavamo.
T'intanavi il corpo
nel mio corpo,
braccia su braccia,
la tua testa sopra il mio cuore,
il tuo calore dolce.
Che cosa è successo?
Dove sei?

SICILIANA

Take the Song

Take the song
the song will save you
Not woman,
who moans for hay
and coverlet
Not time,
that twists us into virtue
and death
Take the song
the ocean and the wind
and swim in it.

LA CANZONE

Prendi la canzone
la canzone ti salverà.
Non la donna,
che gemita per fieno
e coperta da letto
Non il tempo,
che ci torce verso virtù
e morte.
Prendi la canzone
l'oceano e il vento
e nuotaci.

The Poet Dreams of Being Water

It's the energy
and the fluidity
of the thing,
the wave's wing,
the current's swing.

Il poeta sogna d'esser acqua

E' l'energia
è la fluidezza
della vita,
l'ala dell'onda,
l'oscillazione della corrente.

Why Complain

Why complain
of being alone,
of not having love?
All is love,
the song of the wind
in the sea,
the white circles
of sea gulls,
my daughter's smile
as she dreams.

Perchè lamentarmi

Perchè lamentarmi
d'esser solo,
di non aver amore?
Tutto è amore,
la canzone del vento
nel mare,
i cerchi bianchi
dei gabbiani,
il sorriso di mia figlia
nel suo sognare.

Sunset

    The colors of sunset have left
      leaving a silver dying day.
      Light. Light of cloud lines,
        sky of ice channels.

Tramonto

    Sfumano i colori del tramonto
lasciando un giorno argenteo e morente.
    Luce. Luce di linee, di nuvole,
      cielo di canali ghiacciati.

ABOUT THE AUTHOR

Emanuel di Pasquale was born in Ragusa, Sicily, and emigrated to America in 1957. He earned a Master of Arts from New York University in 1966. Since then, he has taught college English. His translations from the Italian include *Sharing a Trip* by Silvio Ramat (2000); *Infinite Present* (co-translated with Michael Palma, 2001); *The Journey Ends Here* by Carlo della Corte; and *Between the Blast Furnaces and the Dizzyness* by Milo De Angelis. His poetry books in English include *Genesis* (1989), *The Silver Lake Love Poems* (2000), *Escapes the Night* (2001); *Cartwheel to the Moon* (2003), and *Writing Anew: New and Selected Poems* (2007). Sections of his book *Genesis* were translated into Italian by Carmela Muscarà (with an introduction by Giovanni Occhipinti) with the title *Un'ambra prigioniera* (2002). He lives in front of the Atlantic Ocean with his daughter, Elisabeth Raffaela.

AWARDS: Bordighera Poetry Prize for translating Joe Salerno's *Song of the Tulip Tree* into Italian (1998); Academy of American Poets' Raiziss/de Palchi Fellowship for translating Silvio Ramat's *Sharing a Trip* into English (2000); Chelsea Poetry Award for *Connections: Prose Poems of Rome, Sicily, and Venice* (2002); National Italian American Foundation grant for translating contemporary Italian poets into English (2002).

ABOUT THE ILLUSTRATOR

Rocco Cafiso is a revered artist and spokesperson in his native Ragusa, Sicily. His work is widely recognized for its cultural vitality and has been exhibited to critical acclaim in Sicily and Italy.

ABOUT THE EDITOR

Salvatore Licitra, a native of Ragusa, Sicily, is professor of International Languages at the Università degli Studi di Catania at Ragusa Ibla. He is author of the book *Quaderni di guerra*, based on interviews with military veterans of World War II; a second compilation will be published under the title *La guerra di Crispinu*.

VIA FOLIOS
A refereed bok series dedicated to the culture of Italian Americans in North America.

NATALIA COSTA, ED., *Bufalini*, Vol. 59, Poetry

RICHARD VETERE, *Baroque*, Vol. 58, Fiction

LEWIS TURCO, *La Famiglia/The Family*, Vol. 57, Memoir, $15

NICK JAMES MILETI, *The Unscrupulous*, Vol. 56, Humanities, $20

BASSETTI, ACCOLLA, D'AQUINO, *Italici: An Encounter with Piero Bassetti*, Vol. 55, Ital. Studies, $8

GIOSE RIMANELLI, *The Three-legged One*, Vol. 54, Fiction, $15

CHARLES KLOPP, *Bele Antiche Stòrie*, Vol. 53, Criticism, $25

JOSEPH RICAPITO, *Second Wave*, Vol. 52, Poetry, $12

GARY MORMINO, *Italians in Florida*, Vol. 51, History, $15

GIANFRANCO ANGELUCCI, *Federico F.*, Vol. 50, Fiction, $15

ANTHONY VALERIO, *The Little Sailor*, Vol. 49, Memoir, $9

ROSS TALARICO, *The Reptilian Interludes*, Vol. 48, Poetry, $15

RACHEL GUIDO DE VRIES, *Teeny Tiny Tino's Fishing Story*, Vol. 47, Children's Literature, $6

EMANUEL DI PASQUALE, *Writing Anew*, Vol. 46, Poetry, $15

MARIA FAMÀ, *Looking For Cover*, Vol. 45, Poetry, $12

ANTHONY VALERIO, *Toni Cade Bambara's One Sicilian Night*, Vol. 44, Poetry, $10

EMANUEL CARNEVALI, Dennis Barone, Ed., *Furnished Rooms*, Vol. 43, Poetry, $14

BRENT ADKINS, ET AL., EDS., *Shifting Borders, Negotiating Places*, Vol. 42, Proceedings, $18

GEORGE GUIDA, *Low Italian*, Vol. 41, Poetry, $11

GARDAPHÈ, GIORDANO, TAMBURRI, *Introducing Italian Americana*, Vol. 40, ItalAmer.Studies, $10

DANIELA GIOSEFFI, *Blood Autumn/Autunno di sangue*, Vol. 39, Poetry, $15/$25

FRED MISURELLA, *Lies to Live by*, Vol. 38, Stories, $15

STEVEN BELLUSCIO, *Constructing a Bibliography*, Vol. 37, Italian Americana, $15

ANTHONY J. TAMBURRI, ED., *Italian Cultural Studies 2002*, Vol. 36, Essays, $18

BEA TUSIANI, *con amore*, Vol. 35, Memoir, $19

FLAVIA BRIZIO-SKOV, ED., *Reconstructing Societies in the Aftermath of War*, Vol. 34, History, $30

TAMBURRI, ET AL., EDS., *Italian Cultural Studies 2001*, Vol. 33, Essays, $18

ELIZABETH G. MESSINA, ED., *In Our Own Voices*, Vol. 32, Italian American Studies, $25

STANISLAO G. PUGLIESE, *Desperate Inscriptions*, Vol. 31, History, $12

HOSTERT & TAMBURRI, EDS., *Screening Ethnicity*, Vol. 30, Italian American Culture, $25

G. PARATI & B. LAWTON, EDS., *Italian Cultural Studies*, Vol. 29, Essays, $18

HELEN BAROLINI, *More Italian Hours*, Vol. 28, Fiction, $16

FRANCO NASI, ED., *Intorno alla Via Emilia*, Vol. 27, Culture, $16

ARTHUR L. CLEMENTS, *The Book of Madness & Love*, Vol. 26, Poetry, $10

JOHN CASEY, ET AL., *Imagining Humanity*, Vol. 25, Interdisciplinary Studies, $18

ROBERT LIMA, *Sardinia/Sardegna*, Vol. 24, Poetry, $10

DANIELA GIOSEFFI, *Going On*, Vol. 23, Poetry, $10

ROSS TALARICO, *The Journey Home*, Vol. 22, Poetry, $12

EMANUEL DI PASQUALE, *The Silver Lake Love Poems*, Vol. 21, Poetry, $7

JOSEPH TUSIANI, *Ethnicity*, Vol. 20, Poetry, $12

JENNIFER LAGIER, *Second Class Citizen*, Vol. 19, Poetry, $8

FELIX STEFANILE, *The Country of Absence*, Vol. 18, Poetry, $9

PHILIP CANNISTRARO, *Blackshirts*, Vol. 17, History, $12

LUIGI RUSTICHELLI, ED., *Seminario sul racconto*, Vol. 16, Narrative, $10

LEWIS TURCO, *Shaking the Family Tree*, Vol. 15, Memoirs, $9

LUIGI RUSTICHELLI, ED., *Seminario sulla drammaturgia*, Vol. 14, Theater/Essays, $10

FRED GARDAPHÈ, *Moustache Pete is Dead! Long Live Moustache Pete!*, Vol. 13, Oral Lit., $10

JONE GAILLARD CORSI, *Il libretto d'autore, 1860–1930*, Vol. 12, Criticism, $17

HELEN BAROLINI, *Chiaroscuro: Essays of Identity*, Vol. 11, Essays, $15

PICARAZZI & FEINSTEIN, EDS., *An African Harlequin in Milan*, Vol. 10, Theater/Essays, $15

JOSEPH RICAPITO, *Florentine Streets & Other Poems*, Vol. 9, Poetry, $9

FRED MISURELLA, *Short Time*, Vol. 8, Novella, $7

NED CONDINI, *Quartettsatz*, Vol. 7, Poetry, $7

ANTHONY TAMBURRI, ED., *Fuori: Essays by Italian/American Lesbians and Gays*, Vol. 6, Essays, $10

ANTONIO GRAMSCI, P. Verdicchio, Trans. & Intro., *The Southern Question*, Vol. 5, SocCrit., $5

DANIELA GIOSEFFI, *Word Wounds & Water Flowers*, Vol. 4, Poetry, $8

WILEY FEINSTEIN, *Humility's Deceit: Calvino Reading Ariosto Reading Calvino*, Vol. 3, Crit., $10

PAOLO A. GIORDANO, ED., *Joseph Tusiani: Poet, Translator, Humanist*, Vol. 2, Criticism, $25

ROBERT VISCUSI, *Oration Upon the Most Recent Death of Christopher Columbus*, Vol. 1, Poetry, $3

Published by Bordighera, Inc., an independently owned not-for-profit scholarly organization that has no legal affiliation to the University of Florida, the John D. Calandra Italian American Institute, or State University of New York at Stony Brook.

www.ingramcontent.com/pod-product-compliance
Lightning Source LLC
Chambersburg PA
CBHW061304040426
42444CB00010B/2506